GREECE AND THE BLACK FLAG

A Little History of Hellenic Anarchy

© Freedom Press

Edited by Rob Ray

Published 2022

ISBN 978-1-904491-42-2

Published by
Freedom Press
84b Whitechapel High St,
London
E1 7QX
freedompress.org.uk

CONTENTS

INTRODUCTION

Produced to accompany Freedom Press's publication of *A Normal Life, Greece and the Black Flag* looks at the broad movements of Hellenic anarchism.

Most of this pamphlet consists of a high-speed trip through the two main phases of libertarian activity.[1] First, the early period prior to the rise of Leninism from mid-19th century through to the 1920s, and then the modern period starting at the turn of the 1970s.

Greece occupies a unique position in Europe, as its modern libertarian movement emerged, to all intents and purposes, fresh-faced from the Athens Polytechnic uprising of 1973 with little historical baggage. In his 2016 study *Anarchy in Athens* Nicholas Apoifis pointedly notes one anarchist activist, Helena, saying "Don't waste your time writing about the other rubbish ... this moment [1973] is the start of our history." Her view reflects a widespread attitude of looking forwards, rather than back.

1   While an argument can be made for including ancient Greece as well, given the word "anarchy" first appears in *Seven Against Thebes* in 467 BC, analysis of libertarian and non-hierarchical thinking in Cynicism, Stoicism etc has been far more comprehensively done elsewhere.

But this is not to say that the anarchist movement had no presence in Greece before that uprising. In fact anarchism had an earlier presence than Marxism, with its most influential essays coming from translations of Mikhail Bakunin, Peter Kropotkin and Jean Grave beginning in the 1860s — Marx and Engels weren't translated until 1893. In 'Before the Junta' we look at the catalysing effects of the Paris Commune and Italian political refugees on a populace that wavered between liberal capitalism and feudal modes, how urban propagandists tried to build rural links and direct actionists assassinated elites before the movement was buried below Bolshevism.

This is followed by a piece on the Athens Polytechnic Uprising, taken from a 2009 edition of *Freedom* newspaper, which explains the iconic importance of that moment in 1973-4 when students stood up to a military Junta and helped precipitate its downfall.

But it's Greece's modern period, with its years of anti-globalisation, economic crisis and migrant struggles, which clearly has the most extraordinary tale to tell, covering the decades since anarchism re-emerged alongside the banners of the university rebels. From early days establishing the stronghold of Exarchia to the growth of black bloc tactics and Europe-leading tendencies towards riot, even terror, no other country in Europe is so intimidating to try and understand in its anarchist movement's relationship to ongoing political crisis.

The history of Greece's squatted social centre scene alone would fill more space than has been set aside for this short overview, and we cannot pretend to cover everything or necessarily put every action in its proper context. Instead, *Greece and the Black Flag* offers a rapid overview of the last 160 years, alongside an overview of groups active in the movement as of 2021.

The pamphlet is bookended with an open letter by Giannis Dimitrakis, the anarchist bank robber who was originally supposed to help write the foreword for *A Normal Life* before he was injured in a prison attack. While this booklet doesn't focus specifically on the phenomenon of anarchist bank robbery in Greece, his letter offers a useful insight into the mentality of the illegalists whose spirit of revolt infuses and drives the history charted in these pages.

~ **Rob Ray**
2021

BEFORE THE JUNTA

In the period prior to and following its successful 1821 war of independence against the Ottoman Turks, Greece went through a similar tale of rapid change in the wake of collapsing feudalism to much of the rest of Europe.

Enlightenment ideas had been finding their way into Greek society through the prior century and a working class was starting to emerge from the artisanal, merchant and landworking classes, producing conditions that would fuel the rise of socialist and anarchist ideas. In the opening decades of the 19th century, for example, a near-identical movement to that of the machine-resistant Luddites could be found in the Thessalian region, centred around Ampelakia which became the hub of a major early co-operative movement. Meanwhile in the ruling class the decentralised, inefficient and slowly crumbling administrative apparatus of the Ottoman empire was being replaced by a more dynamic, home-grown bourgeoisie.

A more formally philosophised understanding of anarchist ideology began to filter into Greece a little way after it was first outlined in Proudhon's *What is Property?*, primarily via Italian propagandist workers and political refugees who brought ideas about trade unionism and internationalism into the north-western Peloponnese. Its most notable early splash in Greek literature was made via an essay titled 'Anarchy' which was published in a satirical newspaper, *Fos*, by Sophocles Karydis on September 9th, 1861. Authorities were immediately incensed by the article, and the author, who had used the pen-name Municipality of Papathanassicu[2] was immediately imprisoned.

At around the same time, with the Greek King Otto[3] trapped between deep unpopularity at home and his reliance on balancing the demands of his Western imperial backers, social conditions were proving fruitful for a new wave of rebellion. A year later, at least one anarchist group, comprising figures such as merchant radical Emmanuel Dadaoglu, Italian

2   The real author was most likely Demosthenes Athanassiou (1830-1878). Born in Portaria, he settled in Athens aged 22 and began writing for Athenian journals in the 1850s before *The Messenger* in 1859. He became an associate editor at *Filo* in 1861. An ardent Proudhonist with individualist leanings, he went on to also publish *Nea Genea* and eventually *Mellon* in the 1870s. Another possibility might be Dimitrios Paparrigopoulos.

3   Otto Friedrich Ludwig von Bayern (1832-62) was installed as a Christian ruler by the Great Powers in 1832 after the Greek War of Independence ended. A Bavarian prince, he was unable to impose himself as absolute monarch and was forced to grant a constitution in 1843. He was replaced in 1863 by a Danish prince, George I (1845-1913).

militant Amilcare Tsipriani and the internationalist Pavlos Argyriadis, drew in anarchist socialists from all over Europe to take part in the riots of 1862 which deposed the monarch. They went on, with fellow influential figure Plotinus Rodokanakis, to try to found an anarchist organisation in Athens, though with limited success.

The anarchists, including Athanassiou through his *Mellon* newspaper, were particularly encouraged in those early years by the Paris Commune of 1871, the grand social experiment which stunned all Europe when the workers ousted their rulers and held out in the city for more than three months. The stridency of the anarchist calls for solidarity again infuriated the ruling class, to the point that an assassination attempt was made on the *Mellon* editor by police on June 3rd of that year, in an ambush at Omonia Square.

In its aftermath, the first sustained anarchist-communist group, The Democratic Association of the People, was founded in Patras in 1876 and, through Italian anarchist Andrea Costa, at the time an ally of the anarchist firebrand Mikhail Bakunin, was represented at the First International in Bern, Switzerland. Opening a newspaper, *Hellenic Democracy*, they were key in maintaining links with the growing movement in Athens where Syros, Aigio, Filiatra and Cephalonia aimed to form a federation. Raided by police that same year, several key figures were arrested and the paper shut down, with the group only being afforded some protection by the presence of socialist Parliamentarians and an intervention by the *Rigas* newspaper. Another club was later opened in Syros which was involved with tannery and shipyard strikes in 1879.

Patras remained the epicenter of anarchist organising for some time to come, with the first truly independent and unflinchingly-titled Anarchist Group of Patras being formed in 1896, publishing *Epi ta pou*. The propagandist group, which had grown out of the city's Socialist Brotherhood, almost immediately ran into trouble when, in the aftermath of the assassination of a banker by anarchist shoemaker Dimitris Matsalis, the paper's entire editorial team was rounded up and sentenced to nearly three years in prison. Nevertheless, the anarchists continued to organise public debates in the city and surrounding villages until 1898 when the group was dissolved amid escalating repression, while focus switched away from the big city towards agricultural workers through the Anarchist Club of Pyrgos, Corinthia, in the western Peloponnese. In a report, the group described its experience:

"Anarchism appeared here in 1892. The propaganda of our ideas took on great proportions, and if we did not have to deal with the issue of religion it would have been even greater ... We do not have authoritarian socialists here: there are only conservatives, liberals and anarchists ... We do not have trade unions, because there is no industry ... only Corinthian raisins are grown and the workers who cultivate the vines are not locals, but come from the neighbouring mountainous areas three times a year, a fact that prevents us from propagating our ideas."

Certainly the mountainous geography and seasonal economy of Greece did not aid in the dissemination of anarchist ideas beyond their core city circles. However the heavily cultivated area, farmed for its grapes and raisin production since at least 75AD, had been in a state of ongoing economic upheaval. During the Greek War of Independence the retreating Turks had burned much of its croplands, with recovery taking decades and only finding prosperity again in the 1860s. Through to 1890 the region became a vanguard of Hellenic commerce, accounting for up to 75% of exports and underpinning national capital growth.

But in 1893-1905 demand for Greek raisins dried up, causing an immediate overproduction crisis. This loss of the "black gold rush," affecting hundreds of thousands of smallholders, caused what became known as the raisin war. Government edicts failed to impact on declining incomes for increasingly poverty-stricken farmers, and villages quickly became unruly, with large mobilisations taking place.

The newspaper *Acropolis* noted that "in Pyrgos and in Ilia in general ... no court decision is executed, no bailiff dares go to execute it, even if accompanied by an entire battalion of gendarmes."

There's a recognisable element of the less successful wing of international anarchist praxis — or lack thereof — peeking through these two descriptions, the frustrated propagandists amid a mobilised peasantry. The travelled zealot, often espousing "advanced theory" to a smallholder who may well be angry, but is no more willing than prior to take instruction from some outsider on how to revolt, less still why.

Where anarchism did make inroads among the peasantry, for all its traditions of social banditry and anti-Ottoman rebellion, it was often corralled within and used to bolster notions of existing social tradition. In a thoughtful 1994 essay, 'Anarchism and social protest in late 19th century Peloponnese', sociologist Manolis Houmerianos notes that for farming populations at the time:

"... anarchist discourse was projected through moral, and religious, values recognisable to the traditional world. In times of turmoil, these values work to cohere local communities as they draw from a common past and culture. Local rights, as understood by a local community, are universalised as 'eternal' traditional values superseding formal State mechanisms that they haven't the power to formally challenge."

"Violent actions legitimised through 'universal' values are not seen as subversive, aimed at abolishing existing norms, but as reaffirming the ability of the local community to have their say. It is not the will to overthrow, but a reminder that they could do so.

"Thus they justify violent attacks mounted against the police in order to recapture churches in villages of Ilia, which had been sealed because they served as gathering places for the insurgents. The legitimacy of the State's repressive measures is questioned, but not the framework that defines them ... On the other hand, this process also offers new elements of social organisation to the producers, as was seen several years later with the establishment of agricultural cooperatives across the region."

Such limited success in the countryside was overtaken by circumstance the following year, as in 1897 the Unfortunate War began, with Greece unsuccessfully trying to push the Ottomans out of Crete, only being saved by an intervention from the Western European powers. Notable in this period was the involvement of 3,000 primarily Italian fighters on the Greek side, among them socialists and anarchists. The Legion of Death, comprising around 80 young anarchists led by Amilcare Cipriani, was the first Italian corps to take part in the invasion of Macedonia.

The last of the groupings to emerge around the end of the century, the Anarchist Workers' Union of Athens, was shortlived, though was able to send a report to the Anarchist International Congress held in Paris in 1900 before its dissolution.

The 1900s themselves saw little in the way of direct organising on the peninsula with two major exceptions, both related to Propaganda of the Deed (lethal, spectacular direct action) strategies.

First was the Boatmen of Thessaloniki, at the time technically rebelling against their still Turkish overlords (the Ottomans wouldn't relinquish control of the city until November 1912), formed from a primarily Bulgarian grouping radicalised by Slavi Merdzhanov. The organisation was active in a campaign of bombings between April 28th and May 1st 1903 against Ottoman oppression. Most notable was their sinking of the French ship Guadalquivir on the first day of the operation, followed on April 29th by the bombing of electrical and water utilities, which plunged the city into darkness. In the aftermath a vengeful Turkish pogrom wiped out many Bulgarians across the city.

Second, a decade later was the action of Alexandros Schinas (1870-1913). It's unclear whether Schinas was an anarchist in sum (though he declared himself a socialist), but the 43-year-old was responsible for the assassination of King George I, leading to the succession of Constantine I which set the stage for major conflicts between the new, assertive monarch and Greek Parliament.

This action marked the eclipsing of anarchism after an active early movement, and what remained was largely destroyed in the post-1918 period as the triumphant Leninist project began to dominate radical thinking. The last organised appearance of the Greek anarchist movement in the 1920s was that of anarcho-syndicalist interventions by K. Spera, G. Fanouraki and others at General Confederation of Greek Workers congresses, as well as with actions by the anarchist-communist Stavros Kouchtsoglou who stridently opposed the new Communist-affiliated unions of the SEKE and KKE. Kouchtsoglou would remain an influential figure in helping to form the cigarette makers' unions in 1921-22. Intermittently Greek anarchists would emerge elsewhere — their exiles and internationalists were numerous in the ranks of the Ukrainian Makhnovshchina, for example, and during the bloody Thessaloniki general strike of 1936 anarchist fighter Giannis Tamtakos was in the thick of things.

As the KKE rose to prominence and became hegemonic on the left in the 1940s, through that decade and most of the '50s-60s Greece would see only a rearguard of people keeping the beautiful idea alive. Pandelis Pouliopoulos and Agis Stinas, both former Communists, would be major figures towards the end of this period. Stinas in particular was the most prominent figure in a group called Ergatiko Metopo (Workers' Front) sharing council-communist and anarchist ideas and publishing a magazine of the same name.

References

* *Anarchy in Athens*, Nicholas Apoifis
* The Municipality of Papathanassiou (konstantakopoulos.gr)
* Land and Freedom (landandfreedom.gr)
* Anarchism and social protest in the Peloponnese in the late nineteenth century (ngnm.vrahokipos.net)
* The Italian volunteer socialists and anarchists in the Greek-Turkish war of 1897 (ngnm.vrahokipos.net)
* A fighter's tale of the 1936 uprising in Thessaloniki (ngnm.vrahokipos.net)

ΕΞΩ ΟΙ
ΕΞΩ ΟΣ
ΜΑΤΟ
ΑΛΗΤΕΣ
ΡΟΥΦΙΑΝΟΙ
ΔΗΜΟΣΙΟΓΡΑΦΟΙ

THE POLYTECHNIC UPRISING
1970s-2000

Paradoxically, it wouldn't be until the rise of the far-right military Junta in the latter half of the 1960s that anarchism would reach the hearts and minds of Greece's younger generation. The Junta's coup in April 1967 coincided with the rise of a major influence on both the new wave of Greek anarchism and movements around the world — the situationists.

By that stage the Situationist International was well into its political period, with Guy Debord's massively influential book *Society of the Spectacle* appearing the same year, keying into the rise of student dissent in France. And in May 1968, as Greece's left scrambled to find purchase and regroup against the Junta, the French would showcase a newfound sense of political possibility in struggle that inspired militants worldwide. With students and workers occupying the streets of Paris, word trickled through to Greek rebels who had become thoroughly disillusioned by repressive antics from the USSR, particularly in the wake of its brutal crushing of Hungary in 1956.

Alongside this phenomenon came direct actions by groups like the Red Army Fraction, Red Brigades, and Operaismo which swept Italy just across the sea — a chaotic assortment of influences which inspired the new anarchism appearing at the tail end of 1971, primarily among young students with little connection to anything which had gone before.

The first tangible signs of this new presence were the establishment of a publishing and political group, International Library, in Athens that year featuring, among others, Agis Stinas, and the founding of Act, a publishing group in Thessaloniki. In Athens Polytechnic, anarchists Stelios Vassiliadis and Angela Fotinou were prominent in a March student strike in the engineering department in March 1972.

Heavy repression from the Junta immediately followed, with Stelios infamously being badly tortured by Junta thugs, leaving him with a broken jaw, torn out nails and crushed genitals. A number of anarchists in this burgeoning movement were handed long prison sentences on top of these intimidation tactics, but by 1973 it became apparent that every effort to interfere in the student unions had failed. Resistance was rapidly increasing.

The Events of November 1973
from Freedom no. 7001, January 17th 2009

The Athens Polytechnic uprising in 1973 was a massive demonstration of the popular rejection of the military Junta. The uprising began on November 14th, escalated to an open anti-Junta revolt and ended in bloodshed in the early morning of November 17th.

In its attempt to control every aspect of Greek politics, the Junta had interfered with student syndicalism by banning student elections in universities, forcibly drafting students and imposing non-elected student union leaders in the national students' union, EFEE. These actions created anti-Junta sentiments among students, such as Geology student Kostas Georgakis who committed suicide in 1970 in Genoa, Italy, as an act of protest against the Junta.

The first large-scale public action against the Junta came from students on February 21st 1973, when law students went on strike and barricaded themselves inside the buildings of the Law School of the university of Athens, demanding repeal of the law that imposed forceful drafting of 'subversive youths', as 88 of their colleagues had been forcefully drafted. The police were ordered to intervene and many students were reportedly subjected to police brutality.

On November 14th 1973, students at the Athens Polytechnic (Polytechneio) went on strike and started protesting against the regime. As the authorities stood by, the students, calling themselves the 'Free Besieged'[4], barricaded themselves in and constructed a radio station (using laboratory equipment) that repeatedly broadcast across Athens: "Here is Polytechneio! People of Greece, the Polytechneio is the flag bearer of our struggle and your struggle, our common struggle against the dictatorship and for democracy!" Leftist later-to-be-politician Maria Damanaki was one of the major speakers. Soon thousands of workers and youngsters joined them protesting inside and outside of the Athens Polytechnic.

The student uprising is generally believed to have been spontaneous, started with purely student demands at first, and not orchestrated by any political groups in Greece. Initially, it was condemned by the parties of the Greek left, which had been banned by the ruling Junta. There were suspicions at the time that the uprising was an act of provocation orchestrated by factions within the military regime opposed to the process of political normalisation and would use the uprising to derail it. However, within a few days the student protests in front of the Polytechnic evolved into a clearly political, quite vocal and rather widespread, albeit peaceful, rebellion against the dictatorship. After approximately three days and nights of continuous

4   A reference to a poem by Greek national poet Dionysios Solomos inspired by the Ottoman siege of Mesolonghi.

mass gatherings in front of the Polytechnic, the protests were put down by force, through the use of tanks and army units which stormed the building during the night of November 17th.

Prior to the crackdown, the city lights had been shut down and the area was only lit by the campus lights, powered by the university generators. In unclear footage clandestinely filmed by a Dutch journalist, a tank is shown bringing down the main steel entrance to the campus to which people were clinging. Documentary evidence also survives, in recordings of the 'Athens Polytechnic' radio transmissions from the occupied premises. In these a young man's voice is heard desperately asking the soldiers (whom he calls 'brothers in arms') surrounding the building complex to disobey the military orders and not to fight 'brothers protesting'. The voice carries on to an emotional outbreak, reciting the lyrics of the Greek National Anthem, until the tank enters the yard, at which time transmission ceases.

On November 25th Taxiarkhos Dimitrios Ioannides used the events as a pretext to stage a counter-coup that overthrew Papadopoulos, and put a dramatic end to Papadopoulos and Spyros Markezinis' attempt for a transition to democratic rule. General Dimitrios Ioannidis arrested Markezinis, cancelled the elections, and fully reinstated martial law.

His regime in turn crumbled in July 1974, after the coup against Makarios III, instigated by Cypriots in contact with the Greek Junta, led to the Turkish invasion of Cyprus.

According to an official investigation undertaken after the fall of the Junta in 1974, no students of Athens Polytechnic were killed during the incident. Total recorded casualties amount to 24 civilians killed outside Athens Polytechnic campus. These include 19-year-old Michael Mirogiannis, reportedly shot and killed by officer G. Derdlis, high-school student Diomedes Komnenos, and a five-year old boy caught in the crossfire in the suburb of Zografou. The records of the trials held following the collapse of the Junta document the circumstances of the deaths of many civilians during the uprising, although the number of dead remains a subject of political controversy. In addition, hundreds of civilians were left injured during the events.

Ioannides' involvement in inciting unit commanders of the security forces to commit criminal acts during the Athens Polytechnic uprising was noted in the indictment presented to the court by the prosecutor during the Greek Junta trials and in his subsequent conviction in the Polytechneio trial where he was found to have been morally responsible for the events.

The uprising of 1973 is hailed by many as a valiant act of resistance against the military dictatorship and as a symbol of resistance to tyranny. November 17th, the date of the event, became the name of a Greek revolutionary Marxist group (17 November, or 17N) in reference to the uprising. The date remains a national school holiday in Greece during which schools and universities stay closed in remembrance.

In the aftermath of the Junta's collapse, with a new liberal-right government in charge (soon to be replaced by the social-democratic PASOK), the way was opened for anarchists to breathe a little more easily, and though in the mid-1970s they were still relatively few in number, they had the reputation of the Polytechnic to draw on and the stage was set for rapid growth. Publishing groups such as Socialism or Barbarism (1974-79) were able to be much more open about their activities and publish freely. Perhaps most notable in this immediate period however was a symbolic ban on police invasions of university campuses, drawn directly from the legacy of the Polytechnic uprising, which for the next four decades would provide a form of semi-sanctuary for rebellious youth.

The university base of the anarchist movement was a major driver of its growth in the mid to late 1970s, strong influences coming from the autonomous occupations and illegalism happening in Germany tinged with a confrontational streak which led to both a new trend of bank robberies beginning with Theodoros Tsouvalakis, and a wave of occupations and riots starting in 1979. In this period a lot of cultural groundwork was laid with lifestyle anarchism, art and music being produced to cohere an otherwise disorganised movement. Bookstores such as Octopus Press in Exarchia and Rigma in Kokkima began to open, with pubs, record shops and cafes becoming known hangouts in Exarchia. "Organised" anarchism of the anarcho-syndicalist or platformist types were less successful in this period — though examples such as the Council Anarchist Group and the Anarcho-Syndicalist Group can be found, their influence was minimal.

The first identifiably anarchist-run anti-war rally took place on May 4th 1976, calling for a cooling of tensions with Turkey under slogans such as "Turkish workers are our brothers" and "the Aegean belongs to its fish," leading on to a number of other demonstrations, including for solidarity with the Red Army Fraction (RAF). The anarchists were notable at increasingly combative events including in a massive strike and protests against an anti-labour law on May 25th, which saw major clashes and the death of a woman run over by police.

The violence in Athens and 150,000 out on strike marked the first major industrial unrest of the post-Junta era.

***

Repression from New Democracy followed swiftly, with the following year seeing the State push to arrest Giannis Serifis, a member of the insurrectionary Marxist-Leninist 17 November group, together with a number of arrests targeting anarchist publishers and activists. Among those picked out were Kyriakos Vassiliadis (an author, publisher, and brother of Stelios), Nikos Balis (a prolific producer of magazines including *Black Sun, When?* and *Polar Star*), Irodis Bakotis and noted rock singer Nikolas Asimos, linking them to "incitement" over their support for the RAF. The following year Giannis Skandalis, Sofia Kyritsis and her husband Filippas were all arrested, on terrorism and weapons charges, and sent down for long, brutal prison sentences. In the enclave of Exarchia, Athens, meanwhile, as the anarchist presence became prevalent, early police efforts to swamp the area with heroin began.

Such tactics were however no more successful than those of the Junta. Hunger strikes and prisoner organising duly followed from the anarchists, while their supporters on the outside began to organise solidarity for their newly-incarcerated comrades. Exarchia reacted strongly against the police strategy, which over time, helped to fix a strong anti-drugs ethos there. By 1980 the anarchists were in a position to fight back.

Rise of the black bloc and mass squatting

The new decade opened with a bang for the anarchist scene in Athens as a new generation became prominent, often again centering around Exarchia and the Polytechnic on its Western border. For the prior four years, in an effort to rein in the unruly district, parliamentary groups including the Stalinish KKE had banned marches marking November 17th in honour of the Polytechnic occupation from finishing at the nearby US Embassy.

In 1980 however a number of protesters ignored the political edict and went anyway, sparking major clashes with police in which two young men, Stamatina Kanelopoulou and Iakovos Koumis, were beaten to death by the cops' hated MAT unit — the latter while he was sitting in a cafe.

In the aftermath the victims were blamed in Parliament, and not a single officer was ever brought to trial. Infamously, newly-installed president George Rallis would state of the incident that "the Archangel Michael holds a sword in his hands to defend himself against the demons. He does not hold flowers."

In an era where anarchism was still somewhat overshadowed by the Leninists the incident went a long way towards undermining trust in Parliamentary tactics, and around this time the first major occupations began to take place in Exarchia's Valtetsiou, Patisia, Thessaloniki and Heraklion in Crete. Thessaloniki in the north and Patras in the south once again became hubs of activity. By 1984, with social democrats in charge for the first time since the Junta's fall, the growing anarchist presence was seeing a step change when it confronted Jean-Marie Le Pen and the Front National at a far-right gathering in Athens' Caravel Hotel. Amid linked struggles against gentrification in Exarchia, the December confrontation saw the first emergence of the black bloc that would come to be an iconic symbol of resistance, and subsequent police raids arrested 170 people.

A year later, the movement swung into high gear as riots ripped through the country. Three cops were killed in the running battles with an activist, Christos Tsoutsouvis, being shot in retribution. The PASOK government found itself squashed between joint pressure from the right and the Communist Party against austerity measures, and as the annual November march commemorating the fall of the Junta rolled around 100,000 people marched through the streets of the capital. As clashes grew towards the end of the march, molotovs crashed into police lines and gunfire cracked in response. When the smoke had cleared a teenager lay dead in the street.

The police shooting of 15-year-old Michalis Kaltezas catalysed an escalating series of actions by an apoplectic anarchist scene, including the mass re-occupation of the Polytechnic and serious rioting throughout the course of the following year. Conferences and the rapid growth of squatting throughout the city followed, including the opening of Lelas Karagiani, Villa Amalias, Scaramanga and many others, some of which would last for decades. The 1985-87 period is broadly considered a moment in which the Greek anarchist movement came into its own, confirmed as a mix of cell-based, semi-organised rebellious structures with its own ecosystem of squatted social centres, gardens and parks, cafes and living quarters. Through to the nineties, this base was a jumping off point for what would became a widespread network of occupations on the one hand and a strong influence from insurrectionist thinking on the other.

Inflation, unemployment and general economic malaise helped push New Democracy over the line again in 1989, ending the PASOK decade with a much expanded anarchist movement that was beginning to expand its field of action, particularly looking at anti-racism, migrant solidarity and the patriarchy. The rise to power of a wannabe Thatcher, Konstantinos Mitsotakis, also provided a significant rallying force as his unpopular privatisation drives inspired considerable opposition, along with the rise of a hard-right opposition in the form of Political Spring taking advantage of a naming dispute over neighbouring (now North) Macedonia. Left and anarchist students were prominent in resisting the measures, with university occupations and street riots being common, and these helped to head off many of Mitsotakis' planned reforms. Writing in *Anarchy in Athens*, the ethnographer Apoifis suggests that this period was when …

"anti-authoritarian and anarchist politics truly came into its own … Once the student of Italian, French and German anti-State radicals, the Athenian anarchist and anti-authoritarian space was now an adult forging its own path. By the early 1990s, it was developing new traditions of direct action with its own martyrs, rituals, successes and failures."

By 1993 Mitsotakis was out and PASOK got back in, slowing confrontation somewhat in the milder climate of the late 1990s. But the direction of travel was clear — Greece would come under increasing pressure from both external and internal political forces to bring its economy under control in the model of neoliberal capital.

In the wake of the privatisation upheavals, incidents of spectacular anarchist political action declined for several years despite occasional standouts, such as a large Polytechnic occupation in 1995 and a campaign of firebombings by the Arsonists of Conscience in 1997-8, but organisation continued with the *Void Network* and *Children of the Gallery* as popular publications. It would be the turn of the Millennium that provided the next major uptick.

References

- *Athens Polytechnic: From small skirmishes to the uprising* (koutipandoras.gr)
- *Organising in Greece 1970-90* (ngnm.vrahokipos.net)
- *1986-87 riots and part 2* (ngnm.vrahokipos.net)
- *Eutopia: Some Notes* (via libcom.org)
- *Anarchy in Athens*, Nicholas Apoifis
- *Freedom Newspaper* (freedomnews.org.uk)

The new century saw a high point for autonomous struggle worldwide as horizontal movements characterised much of the pushback against neoliberalism, which often had bi-partisan support from major electoralist parties.

This manifested through the protest and party scene in Britain, insurrectionist turn of FIJL in Spain and the rise of anti-globalisation movements spanning from Bolivia to South Africa. Perhaps the most famous moments of the period were showcased in the 1999 Seattle and 2001 Genoa anti-G8 protests which marked the beginning and peak of the movement, causing genuine consternation among ruling elites.

Greek anarchism was well suited to involvement in these movements of movements, and was kicked back into gear in 1999 by a successful mobilisation against a visit by US president Bill Clinton. Cars were burned, and the black bloc was getting into full swing. Contingents of Greek militants, taking advantage of the EU's expansion of free movement rights in 1992, were subsequently on the frontlines of several major confrontations between anti-capitalists and State forces trying to protect the international ruling class.

A large contingent travelled to Prague in September 2000, meeting other parts of the European movement as it took on and successfully forced the early closure of a conference of the International Monetary Fund. This was followed by another sizeable showing the following year at Genoa's G8 gathering of wealthy nations in July — perhaps the most violent of that series of flashpoints, where Carlos Giuliani was shot dead by the Italian carabinieri. The fallout from these two events was considerable, and nowhere more so than in Greece, where the experience and its lessons helped forge a new generation of protest veterans.

Importantly, it served to build links with the party and protest movements which had helped produce *Indymedia*, a network of autonomous 'citizen media' outlets, leading directly to the founding of *Indymedia Athens*. Over the next decade *Indymedia* would allow for considerably faster reporting and comment on the movement's many actions, from rallies to manifestos — much to the authorities' chagrin. Even today, with much of the rest of the worldwide Indymedia family having died out, *Athens Indymedia* remains a major news service for the Greek movement, helping to round up the bewildering array of differing and sometimes fractious activist groups making up the broader scene.

In 2002 one of the key moments in modern Greek history took place as it adopted the Euro, retiring the inflation-ravaged drachma and in the process hitching its wagon firmly to German economic interests and dominance. The long-term impact of this decision would be drastic, locking Greece onto a path of privatisation and neoliberalism to service the "largesse" of IMF and EU-financed loans which held a constant threat of ruin over lawmakers' heads if they failed to carry out endless rounds of austerity and sales of national assets. Resistance against this process would help to sustain the Greek anarchist movement right the way through the 2000s and much of the 2010s as the fight for working conditions and public sector jobs heated up, particularly after the US sub-prime mortgage crisis of 2007.

The moment of the global financial crisis, which brought such matters to a head and plunged Greece into a deep financial crisis from which it is still yet to recover, was preceded however by an independent strand of growth from the anarchists. In the year of the Euro's adoption, the most famous name of Leninist militant resistance, 17 November, was formally shut down when its leader Dimitrios Koufontinas gave himself up, however it also saw the founding of the Anti-Authoritarian Current (AK), in preparation for an upcoming EU Council summit which was to be led by then-Greek president Kostas Simitis.

AK's activities were stunningly successful and when the summit took place in Thessaloniki in 2003 the movement was able to turn out 3,000 black bloccers at a time domestically. These were unheard of numbers not just for the Greek movement but across Europe, and the momentum from this militant showing was enormous. That same year the urban guerrilla cell Revolutionary Struggle was founded, announcing its presence with the bombing of an Athens courthouse alongside a manifesto in satirical magazine *To Pontiki* in which it declared itself an anarchist anti-globalisation group.

Over the following three years multiple issues helped keep up the tempo within the anarchist movement. New Democracy's victory in the 2004 elections and the coming of the Olympic Games to Athens offered a solid base for anarchists to go after — both a right-wing government and the widening mess around hyper-exploitation of immigrant workers who had been brought in to help finish Olympic facilities. This was followed by a series of political corruption scandals involving plundered pension funds.

The event of the Olympics was useful for the growth in Athens particularly of a hitherto lesser influence within Greek anarchism — its green and ecological wing. The destructive tendencies of the Olympic bandwagon had been a target of northern European and US green activism for some years prior, and Athens saw an influx of campaigners linked to organisations such as the Animal Liberation Front and Earth Liberation Front, which helped embed ideas around social ecology.

AK continued to grow with the establishment of the Nosotros Free Social Space in Exarchia, mostly run by AK while providing space for publishing *Babylonia* as well as *Void Network*. The "mainstream" anarchist space was of a different type from insurrectionary wing activities, and provides rooms for language classes, skill shares and music events. More generally, Greece's increasing position as a pole of anarchism in Europe, along with its vibrant and capacious squatting scene, drew in support and influences from all over, helping to fuel a diverse and well connected movement.

It's also worth highlighting the Europol report for 2007, which offers a specific aside that "the number of (left wing and anarchist) terrorist attacks rose rapidly towards the end of 2006," suggesting that this period independently produced the beginnings of what was to become a long decade of war against the State.

Of the 55 incidents listed as terror attacks by Europol that year, a full 25 took place in Greece alone. Diplomatic buildings, police forces, vehicles, politicians' offices, banks and surveillance cameras were all on the list of targets, spilling over into the start of 2007 with a rocket attack against the US embassy in January and an attack on a police station in Ionia in April, both claimed by Revolutionary Struggle.

Then, however, came the crash. And everything went into overdrive.

Death of a 15-year-old

In 2007, a mortgage crisis in the US exposed the entire global financial system to potentially catastrophic losses. Financial giant Lehman Brothers went under and massive bailouts had to be found for the banks.

Greece was particularly badly placed to ride out the recession that followed. While it had seen the Eurozone's fastest growth rate from 2000-2007 and seemingly stabilised its economy through the 2000s, the stimulus used to underpin the situation had been debt-driven, with government budget deficits reaching more than 10% of GDP and growth hitting the buffers as the crisis deepened.

Two of the country's biggest industries, tourism and shipping, were hard hit by the global downturn and tax revenues were weak. By 2008 the collapse saw unemployment hitting 25%, and pressure began to build for "fiscal responsibility measures" — austerity cuts and privatisation. Protests began to erupt and, as had become a tradition, grew towards the end of the year.

On December 6th, with tensions running high, police officers set Greece aflame. The December 20th issue of *Freedom* reported:

> Greek society has been shaken to its core this month as thousands of workers. students and immigrants took to the streets to the avenge the murder of a 15-year-old boy shot in the heart by police. Alexandras Grigoropoulos was killed during a minor confrontation with police in the Exarchia district of Athens, an area populated with social centres that historically was a centre of resistance to the military Junta.
>
> The murder immediately provoked the wrath of the Greek anarchist movement, who were joined in the streets of every city by thousands of citizens building barricades, attacking police stations and battling police in riots which paralysed the entire country.

More than 6,000 people turned out for the young boy's funeral, with riot police provoking and attacking the crowd before ultimately teargassing funeral attendees.

The focus of the anger has now shifted from the murder to broader social issues with demonstrations highlighting police brutality, the government's mishandling of pensions and high levels of unemployment.

As rioting entered its fifth consecutive day on Wednesday 10th December a symbolic one-day general strike, originally called in protest at the government's incompetent handling of the economic crisis, brought the country to a standstill.

Intense fighting with protesters of all ages armed with molotovs, cobblestones and crash helmets has gripped the entire nation, with focus points around the main universities in Athens and Thessaloniki.

The occupied universities are now serving as central organising hubs for the demonstrations, thanks to the Greek law of sanctuary, which prevents any police or state forces from entering their grounds.

While one student assembly has already passed a popular vote for the 'violent overthrow of the government', a statement by a group calling itself the 'Occupied School of Theatre' has further explained the position of the students and anarchist revolutionaries.

"This is a generation that has been systematically excluded from any means of expression, deprived of any possibility to decide for itself at school, at university or at work, through its growing alienation," the statement, entitled 'We are at war', began.

"As long as there is no justice, there will be no social peace. We are out on the streets as part of this society but also as part of this social rage. We do not seek to be the leaders of this discontent, we are not experts in violence. We are out on the streets because we are on Alexandros's side. We know well, from our everyday experience in social and labour struggles, in the struggles of immigrants for dignity, in the struggles of the marginalised and the prisoners for a glimpse of freedom, that the State and the institutions of power have always confronted us with the finger on the trigger. We do not just feel hurt, outraged and revolted by the unjust death of a young person. We are also fully aware that, whether we are friends, parents or relatives, for each one of us and each of our beloved ones, there is a police bullet waiting for its fatal call. The explosive social situation these days could — and should — create the conditions and the consciences for a better future. But it could also create the conditions for accepting and legitimising the use of firearms by the police."

The statement goes on to outline incidents of police openly pointing handguns at protesters, knife-wielding fascists fraternising with riot police and shots being fired by police during the funeral. Leftist parties have come out against the violent demonstrations with Aleka Papariga, Secretary General of the Communist Party of Greece (KKE), dissociating "the justified wrath for the victims of state suppression" from the rioter and backing the government's call for national unity."

In the immediate aftermath of the riots, the Greek movement was electrified. In *Anarchy in Athens* Nicholas Apoifis notes:

"Many of the people I spoke with talked of a collective reinvigoration after December 2008, as well as their own personal renewal in anarchist and/ or anti-authoritarian politics.

The years 2009 and 2010 included numerous occupations in universities, schools, trade union buildings, factories and even the National Opera Hall. There were also hundreds of often daily general assemblies, exploring issues as diverse as anarchist economics, strategies to confront the rise of fascism, and the role of social spaces. Alongside this were countless skill- sharing workshops as well as B- Fest, an anti- authoritarian festival of music, political speakers and activist workshops ... This led one participant, Anna, to describe 2009 and 2010 as a 'time of milk, honey, blood and fire.'"

Groups had been emerging including the anarcho-syndicalist Rocinante, and Conspiracy Cells of Fire which began a wave of arsons and bombings across the country, continuing through to the 2020s, working off a form of insurrectionary individualism. Revolutionary Struggle was again active with strikes against police targets including a bus carrying 19 officers, while Cells of Fire carried out seven attacks, primarily against the military and the Italian embassy. A third group, Sect of Revolutionaries made itself known in February with a communique published in daily newspaper *Ta Nea*, citing Grigoropoulos's death and claiming responsibility for an attack on a police station in

Korydallos — the group would go on to particularly target cops in a two-year spree, including anti-terrorist police officer Nektarios Savvas who was guarding a witness in a case against Revolutionary Struggle. Europol at the time counted six active groups including one signing as the Organisation for the Protection of Proletarian Fighters — a reference to a 1940s resistance group.

Amidst the chaos and unravelling economic situation, the 2009 elections were a foregone conclusion and PASOK once again took charge as the economy tanked in earnest, with credit agencies stripping the government of its A- rating. PASOK's soft left credentials did little to assuage the financial markets internationally, and still less to calm the seething fury of the domestic public. Illegalist activities took off in a big way, with serious incidents happening frequently including occupations of journalists' union offices, riots and raids in Exarchia, the firebombing of a train, a university occupation in Thessaloniki which lasted for months, and attacks on PASOK offices just in the first few months of the year. Police efforts to ban face masks and run raids on social centres across Athens, including the arrest of five alleged Conspiracy Cells of Fire members, did little to nothing to stop the tide, and in October revenge raids began in earnest with one drive-by on a police station in Aghia Pareskevi injuring five cops. November 17th's annual day of rallies and clashes was further joined on December 6th by what was to become a new tradition — heavy rioting and occupations marking the death of Grigoropoulos. By the end of the year Europol would be warning that, along with an increased use of firearms, "Actions by anarchist groups are becoming more violent and sometimes well planned."

NEW DECADE OF REVOLT

If the Third Hellenic Republic had any hopes to put the disturbances of the crisis behind them with the turn of the decade they were comprehensively dashed in January 2010 by bombs which exploded outside Parliament and at the General Bank of Greece in Athens. As the months wore on arson attacks on political and corporate targets became too common to list, while at least four major bomb incidents targeted State, financial and fascist premises — the latter of these reflecting increasing hostilities between the anarchists and the rapidly growing presence of Golden Dawn. A major crackdown involving criminalisation of "advertising and financial support of terror groups" the arrest of six alleged members of Revolutionary Struggle and raids hauling in 12 more suspected Cells of Fire members failed to impact on the chaos, with a new Sect of Revolutionaries underscoring that point when they assassinated journalist Sokratis Giolias in July. Over the course of the year 20 major incidents were reported to Europol's anti-terror division, with half being bombings.

Two events did temporarily slow things down. The first was a bomb which exploded outside the National School of Public Administration, killing a 15-year-old Afghan boy and injuring his mother and sister. The incident, which came after many other demonstrations of the indiscriminate nature of parcel and bag bombs, preceded two years of relative hiatus in bombings. The second, an arson attack again Marfin Bank on May 5th, also caused a great deal of soul searching on the spikier end of the protest scene when three bank employees, still working in the building on the orders of their bosses, were trapped inside and burned to death.

More generally however street clashes had become commonplace against both police and the fascists, with anarchists and migrants being particularly harassed by reactionaries capitalising on the situation to try and whip up popular support. This would include serious clashes during the annual Mayday march, migrant riots later in the month and the bombing of a refugee camp in Patras.

And such incidents were merely one wing of the government's many woes. With prime minister George Papandreou going cap in hand to the IMF straight after being elected and austerity politics looming, the trade unions and powerful farming groups began to wake from their habitual slumber. Mass rallies, road blockades and the first of several general strikes took place into March and on May 5th, which saw a rally of more than 100,000 people through Athens — equivalent to 1/7th of the city's population. During the protest a large breakaway group attempted to storm the Parliament building itself before being turned away by police. In Thessaloniki more riots saw 37 people detained. Rallies, strikes and occupations of a similar scale from the broad left and a newly furious middle class would continue to dog successive governments through the end of the 2010s as Greece struggled with intractable debt and pressures from creditors to enforce ever-harsher forms of austerity.

Lorry drivers' strikes and large rallies continued to be held through June with the number of popular demonstrations rising to their highest levels since the collapse of the Junta, but by now a certain ritualisation of unrest was beginning to occur, with summer being a more sedate period that would be disrupted in October by direct actions that continued through winter, swirling around the key markers of November 17th and December 6th. And so it proved in 2010, kicked off in this case by a police incursion into Exarchia that saw the arrest of a well-known broadcaster — a mess of an attack on free speech that led to the resignation of the police chief. Rallies, a massive prison hunger strike and retaliatory clashes spiked towards the end of the year seeing more than 100 arrests — and the anarchists even acquired a mascot with the first appearances of Loukanikos the riot dog, whose clear ACAB mentality frequently helped rally the rally.

A notable aspect of the above is a focus on violent direct action and the uprising-centric propaganda of what came to be known as riot porn, however it would be unfair to characterise this as the sole or even majority activity of the Greek anarchists through the early years of the crisis. While in Athens the insurrectionary current was often ascendant and certainly more visible than the efforts of anarcho-communists and mutual aiders, direct actions of a less violent type such as food banks, expropriation of goods, solidarity with homeless and migrant groups and the running of social centres were all in full swing.

Groups such as the Eutopia project, Tristero, Libertarian Syndicalist Union and the Federation of Anarchists of Western Greece were all active alongside the work of AK and Rocinante. A good example of the multiple threads that were woven through this period was in the aftermath of the 2008 riots, which among many other acts of solidarity saw £12,000 raised to help rebuild the livelihood of an old lady whose kiosk had been torched. The anarchists were not simple in their role as an oppositional force to State and capital, and in 2011 with eyes being turned to the value of street-level occupation the trend would be towards mass mobilisation.

Tunisia's Jasmine Revolution began on December 18th 2010, with protests following the self-immolation of a desperate street vendor, Mohamed Bouazizi, sparking what became known as the Arab Spring of rebellion. This was swiftly followed by the sharp ramping up of anti-austerity protests throughout Spain in what became known as the Indignados movement, and from September across the English-speaking world via the Occupy movement. Greece was no exception to this trend, and saw a resurgence of popular occupation assemblies amid a wave of massive anti-austerity protests taking place throughout the year, beginning with both general and transport strikes in February which saw serious fighting in Athens' Syntagma Square.

With the government struggling to keep a lid on things and cops frequently trying to intimidate their way into dominance anarchists were usually on the front lines of these events, particularly via a number of occupations of town halls and schools. Even the traditionally more sedate summer was marked by confrontations taking place everywhere from Keratea's anti-landfill struggle to a May general strike across 13 cities, which saw severe police violence in Athens.

Protests continued at the end of the month, Syntagma Square in front of the Parliament building being occupied from May 26th despite heavy rain with daily rallies until June 6th. Thousands of people were involved in the two-week occupation partly organised by the extra-parliamentary group Real Democracy Now and eventually manifesting as The People's Assembly of Syntagma Square. By May 28th tents were being raised and other protests took place in Thessaloniki, Patras and Heraklion, joined a day later by a crowd of more than 80,000 for a day of peaceful pan-Europe rallies. Like its sister occupations in Madrid, London and Wall Street, horizontalism was an influence within the politics of the square, with occupiers' demands including at least one anarchist buzz-word in the call for "direct democracy now" and the use of people's assemblies to allow communities to make their own way. But its direction was otherwise relatively vague, including calls to adopt a new citizens' constitution, refuse to pay national debts and tax the rich more heavily.

Describing the attitude of the anarchists to these events, a writer from the *Void Network* noted:

> "We went to camp at Syntagma with Void Network. We announced this in the weekly anarchist assembly "For the Self-

Organisation of Society," which we had been participating in for three years already. Some of the groups refused to come to Syntagma—they called it petit bourgeois, they kept a distance from it, just watching. Other anarchist, autonomous, and anti-authoritarian groups and individuals stayed at Syntagma all summer. We stayed there too, spreading anarchist ideas and practices among countless desperate people, participating in the organisation of the Athens General Assembly to guarantee that everyone would have an equal opportunity to express himself or herself, to ensure that no political party or ultra-left group could manipulate the decisions, to keep leftists from taking over the movement.

"Other groups came only for the three days of riots. The riots were vast … In the middle of financial collapse, in the middle of inhuman austerity measures, unemployment, and unbelievable state repression … this was one of the best summers of my life."

At its more militant end, the Syntagma occupation was capable of rattling the government, including with a mass surrounding of the Parliament building which essentially locked many MPs inside and forced several to escape by boat on June 1st. By June 5th, the crowds gathering in the square soared to more than 200,000 people and other protests were taking place in cities across Greece, prompting an attempted crackdown by police using water cannon and violent corralling of attendees. However the view of many Greek anarchists is that a moment of possibility was lost in amongst the broadly reformist ideas held by the vast majority of the attending public — ultimately, the true demand was for everything to calm down and for prosperous bourgeois life to be reaffirmed and re-asserted.

This was not going to happen in the immediate term however, as Greece's credit rating slumped to its lowest CCC rank and students became the next to revolt, with occupations of at least 87 university buildings across the country in June against a privatisation-friendly Education Bill, spreading to more than 300 by late September. Direct action groups started reconnecting cut off electricity, trade unionists were marching every week and multiple general strikes took place through October and December alongside workplace occupations and innumerable smaller actions, all tail ended by the annual clashes of November 17th and December 6th. Notable in the autumn and winter period was a direct clash between the anarchists and Communist

KKE, with the latter acting as a last-ditch defence force of the Parliament building itself.

By the end of the year, Papandreau's government was out and a caretaker cabinet led by Lucas Papademos was in, shepherding through a €130 billion loan from the EU and IMF tied to extreme austerity measures. On February 7th this process sparked yet another two general strikes and a round of protests that turned into serious rioting, with 45 banks, cinemas, shops and offices burned to the ground, 25 protesters injured and 40 cops hurt.

Throughout the period anarchists and their migrant allies were also struggling against the rise of Golden Dawn. Largely a busted flush before the crisis, the fascist party grew immensely over this era of revolt and achieved its greatest electoral reach in the 2012 elections, winning 21 seats in opposition to the pro-austerity coalition of PASOK and New Democracy that came to power. The fascists' scooter gangs regularly harassed and attacked anarchist spaces, leading to an escalating series of tit for tat actions. Paramilitary raids were made against migrants' workplaces and even against larger squatted housing blocs such as abandoned factory units, often in tacit cooperation with the police which voted heavily for Golden Dawn and whose own August crackdown detained more than 6,000 people. This would continue into 2013, when the murder of musician Pavlos Fyssas would undermine any pretence Golden Dawn had to respectability.

Anarchists were heavily involved in solidarity work and counter-operations against these attacks, such as the burning of the party's offices in Athens on August 12th, or helping to open, run and protect migrant centres. Self-organised mutual aid groups became increasingly common as the crisis wore on, with food distros springing up in the cities in the face of an official ban and new unions forming.

As the months of revolt rolled round, November was for once relatively quiet other than a 48-hour general strike and fascist-antifa clashes. But on December 6th extensive riots broke out in Exarchia, with a police campaign following on. Raids saw Villa Amalias, one of the oldest squats in Greece having been taken over in 1990, evicted with police claiming that materials to make 1,500 molotov cocktails had been seized. Part of a project to evict 40 squats in total, it prompted a strong response from the anarchists with 150 temporarily retaking the space just a month later.

Clashes over that and other raids led to more than 90 arrests for trespass, and rallies in support of the detainees drew several thousand people. Violent actions began to rise again shortly afterwards, including explosions at journalists' homes and shots being fired at the headquarters of New Democracy.

Tensions were further inflamed when anarchist Nikos Romanos, a close friend of Alexis Grigoropoulos who held the young man in his arms as he died, and three others were arrested for attempted robbery in February 2013. Following their arrest they were beaten by the police so badly that the cops decided to (very clumsily) doctor their pictures prior to giving them to the media. The scandal brought considerable public condemnation and turned the young Romanos into a symbol of police brutality, A year later his hunger strike for the right to an education in prison would bring thousands into the streets to support him.

With strikes and protests still at a high through March and struggling to cope with the unrest, Minister of Public Order Dendias severed the server connection of *Indymedia Athens*, Radio98FM and Radio Entasi on April 11th in an effort to silence the anarchists. But this was a drop in the ocean compared to the momentum of public anger over high unemployment and the prospect of massive public sector job cuts related to bailouts. Farmers, transport workers and teachers were all out in the spring and summer, while for the anarchists, the formation of Rouvikonas as a support group for political prisoners offered a new pole of activity. The group would later grow into a direct action force of more than 60, carrying out regular raids against political targets, and publicly videoing/commenting on their actions. Sitting between the insurrectionism of Revolutionary Struggle and grassroots organising tactics, they are more able to sail under the radar of MAT and courts as their actions are considerably less violent than other groups, targeting property rather than people.

One of the first serious cuts was an odd choice as State broadcaster ERT was shut down, the fanfare of its demise sparking immediate protests, strikes and the loss of coalition partners, causing a government crisis as Papademos' majority shrank to three. By September, a new wave of evictions had sparked an occupation of municipality buildings in Ioannina and Heraklion, and a general strike on September 16th against public sector layoffs. The Athens Metro was shut down by workers the following month.

Alongside the annual protests and riots, November 17th was notable for a drive-by shooting of Golden Dawn members, carried out in revenge for the death of Pavlos Fyssas. Two fascists were killed and one injured in the attack, which was claimed by the Militant Popular Revolutionary Forces.

This was part of a picking up of the kinds of cases that make Europol terror lists, with shots also being fired at the German ambassador's home later in the month. Over the course of the year 14 attacks were linked to Conspiracy Cells of Fire as part of a global initiative known as Operation Phoenix, which illegalists from Greece, Chile, Indonesia, Russia and Mexico participated in as a form of solidarity with imprisoned anarchists. 2013 also saw the debut of Green Nemesis, a food contamination campaign aimed at multinationals in which poison was injected into products in an attempt to force recalls.

The migrant crisis, and Syriza

Positioned on the EU border with Turkey to its east and Libya across the Med, Greece has always been a key migration route and particularly in recent times during what was dubbed the European Migrant Crisis — a fundamentally self-absorbed term for the results of conflicts across the Middle East and Africa.

The rising number of war refugees was first registered in 2010, with millions subsequently fleeing the battlezones of Syria, Iraq and Afghanistan, and for the first few years a chaotic situation in Libya meant that Italy, specifically Lampedusa, was the primary landing site.

In 2015 however, as Tspiras started settling in on his anti-austerity, stand up to the EU ticket, numbers tripled from a year prior with more than a million people crossing the Mediterranean with around 850,000 heading to the Aegean islands and Greece. The government was poorly prepared for this influx of people and several islands, most notoriously Lesbos, had massive, poorly provisioned camps established on them.

Amid widescale fascist activity and facing a police force that was chafing at the bit to lash out at migrants, activists from all over Europe were heavily involved in solidarity work throughout the year-long crisis, both on the islands and mainland.

Solidarity networks saw anarchists heavily involved in the humanitarian work of disembarking and providing for new arrivals, with the most publicly-known initiative being the squatting of formerly abandoned spaces which were turned over to house thousands of migrants, peaking at between 2,500 and 3,000 at a time in 2017.

Several squats, notably Gini, Notara 26 and Themistokleus 58 were run on explicitly anarchist principles, refusing overtures from NGOs and the State to formalise. Others involved anarchist support of refugees to self-organise their own spaces such as Acharnon and 5th School. Feminist squats such as Stephi housed women and children, while City Plaza, established in 2016, worked on a broader base as a political left sphere.

The projects were, of course, beset with difficulties and complications, including an attitude of at best grudging acceptance from city and State authorities, but their flexibility and refusal to patronise consistently wrongfooted and bettered the top-down, underfunded and often dangerously lackluster efforts of Navy-run distribution centres and slow-moving NGOs.

Centering once again on Exarchia, meetings and gatherings were constant between a mix of anarchists, volunteers and refugees, with the latter being backed up with food, medical treatment and supplies while they self-organised their own communal living spaces, set up their own security against fascist attacks and found ways to survive in the longer term.

Tiff Griffin, an English teacher who volunteered at both NGO and anarchist sites, reported in a 2016 blog that in the camps:

> "Social and cultural bonds were utterly broken. The lack of respect for elders is out of place in Islamic culture and, whatever the rights or wrongs of that, for a young Syrian Muslim girl

to spit on an adult man tells you something. The parents had lost control of their lives and were institutionalised, depressed, some of them traumatised. They were infantilised, reduced to passively standing in queues waiting for handouts and food supplied by the Greek Navy that were basically pasta and about a tablespoon blob of tomato sauce. This was the refugee racket of the EU grant chain."

While in Exarchia, by contrast:

"It was like night and day with the NGO camp. The hotel was clean, well run and the children were much better behaved. The parents were in control and getting up at 8.30am. The volunteers worked, cooked and ate alongside the refugees together in solidarity and the food was healthy, traditional Syrian and Greek food. I taught children that were much better behaved and I had support from the parents. I was exhausted and my hands were blistered from cutting carrots for 400 people and I loved it. I was achieving something."

The new Greek government meanwhile was treading water, failing on every front. Having partially demobilised oppositional direct action from the electoral left through its election victory, Syriza found itself presented with exactly the same intractable problems which had done for PASOK. The government's finances were precarious at best and dependent, if unwilling to go into the instant crisis of sovereign default, on the continued goodwill of its IMF and European lenders.

As a result, no real end to austerity was in sight and the 'radical socialist' government was open to attack from both its left and right, accused of profligacy and irresponsible behaviour on the one hand and of failing to relieve squeezed living standards on the other. Without resources, the party swiftly went within months from being the defiant darling of European leftism to signing off the Third Economic Adjustment Programme, accepting another even more aggressive austerity-linked bailout and betraying the results of its own "should we default" referendum in the process.

The party's own former finance minister, Yanis Varoufakis, characterised the decision to do so as "Greece's terms of surrender" and Syriza was thrown into an immediate crisis, triggering a snap election in September in which Tspiras was re-elected with a historically low turnout. Austerity would only deepen on the left's watch.

Similar to the phenomena of electoral left "successes" in Spain with Podemos and Corbynism in Britain, Syriza's rise and failure had broad negative long-term impacts on street mobilisation from the general public, particularly after it became clear that as far as the political class was concerned, there would be no challenging neoliberal economics.

Though everything is relative (as of 2021 Greece continues to average three to four significant strikes a month and had its first pandemic-era general strike in June) the number of violent confrontations dipped significantly. The biggest counter to this malaise took the form of Black December, a concerted anarchist campaign which led to fierce rioting on December 6th.

Illegalists meanwhile continued attacks on sites such as New Democracy's Athens HQ, the house of the Thessaloniki Police Union chief, and the warden of Domokos prison but these were relative outliers. Attacks would remain at lower levels through to the end of the decade, though Europol continued to warn that "left-wing and anarchist terrorist groups have retained their operational capabilities as well as their access to weapons." Notable in this latter period was the continuation of the Green Nemesis actions, which saw iterations Two and Three in 2016-17, as well as continued strikes attributed to Conspiracy Cells of Fire, the Revolutionary Self-Defence Organisation and Group of Popular Fighters.

The near-killing of former prime minister Papademos in his car by a letter bomb in May 2017 seemed to set off particular alarm bells for the State, and 2018, despite the emergence of a new group, Rubicon (Rouvikonas), saw a major wave of arrests, leading to the imprisonment of 45 people the following year. Between 2019 and 2021 most of the serious incidents had subsided with none being recorded during the Covid pandemic.

Elsewhere, much of the anarchist focus in the final years of the 2010s remained on migrant solidarity, which in the 2016-2018 period included a 2016 No Borders camp in Thessaloniki which attracted anarchists from all over Europe, clashing with cops both there and surrounding rural areas. Through the winter of that year and into 2017 solidarity actions and concern over the plight of thousands of people stranded in inhuman camp conditions aimed to support hunger strikes which sprung up and many more police raids, which hit multiple migrant centres in yet another reversal of Syriza's progressive credentials.

The most dangerous end of this work concerned a growing presence of fascist militias however, now relatively decoupled from respectability politics as the far-right's electoral train derailed in the face of pressure from the courts. January 2018 would see the burning of long-running squat Libertatia by a fascist mob in Thessaloniki, the culmination of more than 30 attacks which had taken place over the previous year including by Combat 18 Hellas and Golden Dawn backers.

Neo-nazis continued to heavily target anarchist and migrant squats and in response March 10th saw a major rally against nationalist attacks in Thessaloniki attended by anarchists from across Greece and the Balkans. Attacked by police, it became a major riot and Thessaloniki University was occupied just days before a series of police raids evicted another three squatted centres, on the heels of several other far-right attacks.

Around a dozen major centres existed in Athens at the time, many in the Exarchia area, and Summer remained busy with efforts to hold the network together while finding spaces to replace those that had been cleared.

After a relative quiet patch, winter once again saw considerable mobilisation with a massive November rally despite police intimidation tactics, as well as major riots in Athens and Thessaloniki in December — 118 people being detained en masse in the latter.

The Syriza period, brief as it was, ended in 2019 with the election of New Democracy. Both the left and far-right lost out in an election hinging on ND's pitch that Syriza's answers had failed, there was no alternative and a steady Toryish hand at the tiller was the best to be hoped for. Some ballot-burning incidents aside, 40% of the electorate agreed, removing more than a third of Syriza's seats at a stroke and giving ND an outright majority.

The results, which also wiped out Golden Dawn in Parliament, essentially marked a punctuation point in the most chaotic period of the post-2008 financial crisis.

Taking stock in that year, GDP had crashed from $354.5bn in 2008 to a semi-stabilised level of around $190bn, a sustained fall of 46%. Unemployment continued to struggle to dip below the 16% mark, the worst in the EU. Economic growth was anaemic and average wages had fallen back to levels last seen in the late 1990s — they remain some of the lowest in the EU. Vast government debts had been accrued amounting to more than 200% of GDP, owed mostly to Germany, France, Italy, and the IMF. It was a total victory for neoliberal capital and predatory inter-EU State interests, in which a defeated debtor country with an impoverished population of desperate labour was largely broken to heel.

And now the old guard ruling elite were back, raring to tackle any remaining unruly elements. Under Kyriakos Mitsotakis the New Democracy administration was, from the get go, straightforward on its main target — rebel strongholds.

Prior to the elections, Mitsotakis had made his name on tough-sounding rhetoric about the anarchists, saying in 2018: "Today in Exarchia a new breed of 'fighters' is being groomed who could very easily end up being the new generation of terrorists ... the difference between a Molotov cocktail and a Kalashnikov is actually not so big."

Directly after the July elections he began his campaign, appointing Michalis Chrisochodis — credited with being part of the team that took down N17 in 2002 — as minister for citizen protection and setting Exarchia as a major strategic target for police. Between August and October raids particularly targeting refugee squats evicted more than 500 people from the area, partly to enable a land-grab which it's feared is a precursor to cleansing "gentrification." A campaign in the area from 'Exarchia Tourism' is currently targeting use of housing for Airbnb in an effort to deter such encroachment.

Two members of Rubicon, Nikos Mataragkas and Giorgos Kalaitzidis, were picked up on bogus charges and put into a Kafkaesque nightmare of legislation that was only finally defeated in November 2021, after a two-year campaign by the State to put them away for murder and incitement. Many other anarchists were targeted by similar repressive efforts.

And, casually throwing out a supposed founding principle of the third Hellenic Republic, ND also rushed through a repeal of the law which had for nearly 50 years protected university campuses from police interference, explicitly to prevent anarchists from seeking sanctuary in those spaces.

This was followed, as the pandemic arrived in 2020, by the introduction of new legislation giving police direct powers to control and approve protests in the name of "controlling Covid." These have, of course, been repeatedly used instead to try and end political challenges, with 5,000 cops flooding the streets on December 6th to curtail the annual marking of the death of Alexander Grigoropoulous.

The position of Hellenic anarchism as it faces the rest of the 2020s is precarious. It is under pressure from powerful, driven enemies, isolated in comparison to the fire and mass revolt of the post-2008 period. Finding direction and purchase is a challenge of itself, and resources are stretched. But Greece remains the most rebellious spark of European anarchism.

It has some fight to it yet.

References

- *Athens Polytechnic: From small skirmishes to the uprising* (koutipandoras.gr)
- *Organising in Greece 1970-90* (ngnm.vrahokipos.net)
- *1986-87 Riots* Parts 1 and 2 (ngnm.vrahokipos.net)
- *Eutopia: Some Notes*
- *Anarchy in Athens*, Nicholas Apoifis
- *Athens and The War on Public Space*, Brekke, Fillipidis and Vradis
- *EU Terrorism Situation & Trend Report*, 2007-2020 (europol.europa.eu)
- *Freedom* newswire (freedomnews.org.uk)
- *Unicorn Riot* (unicornriot.ninja)
- Rouvikonas Anarchists 'Open Office' in Greek University (greekreporter.com)
- Riots Flare in Athens on the 10th Anniversary of a Police Killing (nytimes.com)
- How a group of Athens troublemakers goes unpunished (economist.com)
- Anarchists from across the Balkans clash with Greek police (dw.com)
- Muslim Refugees Team Up With Anarchists in an Effort To Shame Greece (theatlantic.com)
- Destination Anarchy! Every Step is an Obstacle (crimethinc.com)
- The Astonishing Story of Greek Anarchists and Syrian refugees (adcochrane.wordpress.com)

A LETTER FROM ANARCHIST GIANNIS DIMITRAKIS

Korydallos Prison,
June 5th 2006

On the afternoon of Monday January 16th 2006 Giannis Dimitrakis took part in an armed heist at the National Bank of Greece in the centre of Athens. After an exchange of fire with two cops from a special unit Giannis was shot three times and seriously injured. The other four robbers managed to get away from the scene with about €50,000, one also being slightly injured.

Giannis, who openly admitted that he is an anarchist, stayed in different hospitals for a few months till he recovered, then was sent to Korydallos prison. In another parody of the Greek justice system Giannis was charged with seven robberies, and numerous counts of attempted murder, topped with the anti-terror law. It's not the first time that a fixed charge has been handed down to anarchists in Greece.

Comrades,

This letter is my first attempt to communicate and comment on the events that I experienced during the bank robbery of the National Bank of Greece on January 16th. Before I expand upon events, I'd like to say a few things regarding my motives in taking such action, and what it meant to me.

Present-day society is a wagon following a predefined course, leading straight towards its complete dehumanisation. The role of its passengers, wheels and horses — in other words of its driving force — is played by us, the people. The wagon's driver has the cruel face of capitalism and its co-driver is a faceless and vague State. The path the wagon follows is of course not strewn with rose petals and flowers, but with blood and human bodies. With individuals or groups of people who wanted to either resist and change its frantic course or to stand as an obstacle in front of it. The list of those is long: insubordinates, rebels, leftists, anti-authoritarians and anarchists fill many bloody pages in this journey's storybook. Somewhere in between the last two groups is where I place myself.

So, to the degree of consciousness that my world-view and perception allows me, what I can easily see is that present-day society relies solely on violence, oppression and exploitation. A society which aims at the loss of human dignity in every way, by all means. This is experienced by each and every one of us in everyday life, either through being forced to deal with State institutions at work, and from those who manage and profit from us.

Employment, work: words whose true meaning is wage slavery, enslavement. Work and its surplus value are the pillars of today's economic system while the individuals that carry it through and the circumstances under which this takes place confirms that people are treated as expendable goods, as modern slaves. We see workers who are rotting away from illnesses due to their long-term exposure to hazardous substances, who die by falls or by explosions in the capitalist temples they are building, losing their urge, their liveliness, their spontaneity — all that characterises a would-be free person.

Working exhausting hours and employed in two or three jobs simultaneously just for a few crumbs. When to cover their most basic needs a person is obliged to mortgage themselves to those cold-hearted oppressors otherwise known as banks, and under the burden of this financial responsibility start showing signs of subservience and submission. Then, in the case that they cannot in the end cope, they are led to bankruptcy and suicide or are publicly ridiculed by the mass media as one more human wreckage.

Leading us to one conclusion.

The State and capital, in order to continue, manufacture modern-day helots (slaves of ancient Greece) who can easily be compared to those of Sparta. A system which sacrifices human lives on the altar of profit callously and audaciously. As previously mentioned, one of the main partners in this crime are banks, which are nothing less than legitimised loan sharks and partly to blame for the plundering that's taking place at the expense of peoples' work.

Taking all the above into consideration we can understand Mack, in Brecht's Threepenny Opera, when he asks: "What is a bank robbery compared to the founding of a bank?"

And then I take myself into consideration, a man wanting to resist on a personal level — as with on a mass level where all who know me personally know I have participated as much as I could — my future yoke. To determine for myself the conditions and quality of my life, to put in to practice my refusal to "work," to play the role of yet one more productive unit, yet another wheel in the wagon.

I wanted to attack the monstrosity that is called a bank (while having no illusions that I'll inflict any major blows to this economic institution), choosing to mark a course of dignity in my life. I decided to rob one. An act which I consider, amongst many others, as revolutionary and which claims deservingly its own place as such.

I must admit that I intended to keep the money I was going to acquire through the robbery. At the same time, however, as an anarchist and someone who wishes to show their solidarity through their deeds, I'd be one of the first to actively and with joy help in contributing to monetary needs which might come up in this scene to which I belong.

Finally, what I'd like to point out here is that all which I have mentioned up to now does not in any way mean that I support a notion that whoever is an anarchist should be a bank robber — or that whoever works is enslaved.

This extract is the first part of a fuller essay on his experience in the robbery, from a pamphlet produced to mark a massive prisoner uprising in 2008 sparked by an attack on Giannis in Maladrino prison. The full text is at anarhija.info/library/wp-textovi-3

Of all the anarchist movements of 21st century Europe, Greece is perhaps the most explosive. From 19th century beginnings, to facing down the Junta's tanks in 1973, to the street war of Greece's 2010s economic crisis, this short history charts a path through its fire, fury and solidarity.

£3.50